Foreward

I'm writing this, rather, I am typing this on a keyboard, connected to a computer, connected to the internet, which has connected me to google docs- so that I may capture a few thoughts to offer to the reader. It is January 7th of 2020, the beginning of a new year. In many ways, it feels like we are the beginning of a new existence. A time where technology and the ecosystem of connected devices, people, networking cables, and colorful pictures on digital screens have had time to germinate into the beginning of a brave new world.

Our existence is perpetually bombarded with the thoughts and opinions of the other pink squishy apes who chose to shout the loudest, but not always honestly. Advanced animals who, for decades, strived and struggled to distance themselves from our animal nature, until it became posh to "get woke" and revert to some contrived, made-up, version of a "natural state". A truthful method to living life defined subjectively by the flawed, fickle, hungover, foggy-minded, overworked, affection-starved critters that brought Facebook, fad-diets, and the goddamn DMV into existence.

I don't intend this glib use of sarcasm to discourage or turn away readers, but to offer context to a collection of beautiful poems. Poems claimed from the cosmos for the benefit of both the author and the people who read them. Poems written for the purpose of processing the vicious and uncertain feelings of youth, and the unavoidable horror of becoming an adult. Poems that help thoroughly analog humans navigate the insane, incongruent reality of all the world's genius, agony, culture, and righteous indignation as they violently collide with one another- the aftermath of that little bit of coaxial cable poking through the floorboards in your house.

The author of these poems represents a sect of humanity that I also belong to. People who grew up in a part of the world that never traveled at the same speed that the rest of humanity did. People who aren't convinced that those with a blue verified check-mark, a podcast microphone, or millions of disposable online drones are the prophets and priests of the new world order. New religions plague and harass our generation with morality games and the terrible curse of too many options. The new reality, it seems, is filled with many Gods.

The thoughts and feelings contained within these pages offer the reader a vision of Man-kind at odds with its own creations. There are thoughts on life and the progression through it, however clumsy and indelicate it may be. There are stories of love, both the sad longing for connection and the joy of true, patient, and silly romance. There are light-hearted observations about the reality of completing life's necessary chores and also the blueprints to a disciplined mind devoted to empathy, rather than brute force, as a means of achieving goals. All are meant to be interpreted metaphorically, literally, seriously, and not-seriously. The point is that there is no point; until we each individually decide there is. May you read this book and enjoy the singular pleasure of allowing your mind and your soul to chew on the most delicious treat of all- perspective.

-Alex M. Barnes

I had thought about having *I Dance* (p.61) take the place of any formal shout-outs but decided that its best if you actually read that one now and then come back...

If you have been a part of my life in any capacity then I owe you my gratitude. Simply being yourself has allowed me the experience and inspiration needed to keep on living, to open my mind, to write and put this book together. No thanks or apologies required I only ask that you read this with appreciation knowing that it would not be possible without you.

Life is a dance and when my life wasn't going how I wanted, I chose to get better at the dance. The crazy dance of life. Its good, bad, ugly, and beautiful. Its non-sense and make-believe and non-stop dedication. Life is a dance that requires your attention and demands your respect!

-Jacob M. Wratten

Preface

I grew up in a very small town. My school had less than three hundred kids, kindergarten through twelfth grade. My own graduating class numbered twenty-six. In my town everyone knows everyone and they don't always get along, but the worst that you can do is be impolite – to openly judge and ridicule.

I promise you, if you stop being impolite people will notice and change will happen. Judgement and hostility will be traded for patience and communication. You will smile at the people you meet and nod in recognition that we do indeed share the same time and small world in this dimension. Faltering here will get in the way of you actually enjoying YOUR life.

Early in my 20's I started listening to an Alan Watts' lectures and heard him talk about individuality like waves in the ocean. Our ocean is our universe broken down into families, towns, cities, religions, our teams, and our friends. Though we may wave and stand out we are still part of this larger thing that is trying to express itself and figure itself out.

We are both sides of the coin. We are individuals, but we are human, and we are here. Right now. I am a Wave in this Ocean and I wave for both of us. For you, out of acceptance, to serve as a confirmation that you are in fact alive and noticed finally, for the being that you are. For myself the reason is the same.

I wave in recognition of me, to the collection of thought, body, and experience that I have become. I wave in celebration that I am able to *be* at all. You are not a social security number, car registration, or ballot lost in this corporate government beast. You simply are, and going forward do you choose to wave in your own way of acknowledgement or do we keep being impolite?

I Wave.

Experience

English 101.........3
Twilight on The Nine Mile.........6
A court Date and an Oxygen Tank.........8
Document 7.........10
Monday.........12
Class #26 April 19th 14
Daylight Savings.........16
April Afternoon.........18
A Syllable Cycle of Life.........20

Thoughts

Introspection.........25
The Truth... As I Recall It.........26
Attentive not Obsessive.........28
Just a Day.........30
Priorities.........32
Racket Outside-in.........34
I Think, I Try, I Create.........36
Grandma B.........38
Something Better.........40
Taking Responsibility.........42
Aside.........43
Homesick.........45
Earth to Jacob.........47
A Good Person Trying to be Better.........50
Self-Discovery.........53
Nature Vs. Nurture.........55
Document 6.........57
Still Boys.........58

Intimacy

Document 3.........60
I Dance.........61
Love Lasting.........63
Only Slowly Goes This.........65
The Good Love.........66
Love Eternal.........68

Lessons

Story of My Life.........71
This Is Growing Up.........72
I Can Cause Seizures.........74
Perspective.........76
My Meditation.........78
Meditation.........79
Condensation.........80
Office life.........83
I Am Sane.........84
I Was A deer Once.........87
The Whole Is Its' Parts.........90
I Am the Leprechaun.........92
Document 2.........94
The Universe.........96

I tried to include the date each piece was written if I could find it. Sometimes I wrote them down and sometimes I didn't. The originals to these are written on bits of cardboard boxes, the backs of receipts from the store, and on old envelopes. I had to write whenever the thought came because it might never come to me like that again. What you read here and what I scribbled down in my trance like state has changed almost not at all. From a young age I didn't really do "drafts" I just tried to go slow and be precise.

For myself the dates are fun because I can think back to how old I was when I wrote it and what I remember life being like then. I think what emotions I must have been feeling and what brought them on. Here, I give them for frame of reference. I was born on July 8th 1987, the first poem I wrote was in August on 2003 and was, looking back, very angsty. Immediately in my head I make excuses for the angst, then I slow myself down and tell my feelings that they need no explanation. I have proof of my own supposed awkwardness in old pictures and poems, a progression of me, and since I like who I am now, I like who I was then too.

Experience

English 101 3/24/2009

Let your scholars pick this apart,
find all of my hidden meanings
destroy another story.
An exaggerated *your* version.

You take my poetic license
twist it to fit your parameters,
make it mean slavery or feminism
for youth or change or suicide.

This writing is my suicide
my choice of an acceptable death.
Letting all you people undress
my thoughts with your mind and rape them.

Placing them under lenses
endlessly examining them.
You would torture meaning
from their every fragile syllable.

Such atrocities should never be
inflicted on such innocence as thought.
Just thoughts and why would you beat them
insisting upon knowing deeper meanings.

Probing at the pauses and hyphens
wondering what each break could mean.
Take it in and feel it instead.
If somehow it reaches you then keep it.

>>>

But to hell with you
who try and teach it,
trying to teach my feelings
putting so many words into my mouth.

This is me,
all that you will ever have of me.

Don't try to *interpret* it,
just let these words be and flow.
Keep them safe and untainted.
Keep thought sacred.

I had wanted to be a teacher for at least part of my life and school was what made me change my mind about what and how I taught. I remember hating having to analyze and pull the messages out of books, out of art, and then be graded on it. I thought that method of dissection was out of place I felt that way about myself too. How could these people judge me and not know me? They didn't know my history and my mannerisms, or the ways in which I learned the best. I felt immediately at odds.

What I missed was creator commentary. I needed and wanted more information. I wanted the big picture and still do now. I want to know current events and stereotypes and slang, I need that. The work is not stand alone and is subject to the times and the bias of its creator. My hope is to give you some sort of inside look, some preface or afterthought, which may not have been fully realized or appreciated by myself at the time. We judge each other harshly instead of appreciating each other genuinely.

Twilight on the 9 mile

The fog rolls out
from the swamp tonight.

And the Dark,
it is indifferent.

I will be busy
doing human things,
animal things,
everyday things.

Under the watchful
eye of my mother
nature.

I live next to a swamp, as my family has for over one hundred years. The fact that we have not chosen to leave should speak to how fond of it we are. How fond of it I am. We as humans are still some strange combination of hunter/gatherer and herder/farmer. We suffer a disconnect with nature. We have wandered into the world of creation and possibility and forgotten how to get home. We have forgotten how to live with balance and the concept of enough. Looking out across the field, into the quiet inhales and exhales of this swamp I see that we are somehow the same. We exist in the same time and space and it is ordinary and *spectacular*.

A court date and an Oxygen Tank.

You'd think that she'd go crazy wouldn't you,
With that rhythmic release of a respirator bag?
What about those hoses that run
intruding upon her nasal cavities and resting
menacing and unnatural on her soft upper lip?

Does she forget and move to itch and despair
to find youth has left her with this,
this frail body kept through such ugly
enhancements?
She would feel that small band behind her ears,
with every turn of her head she is reminded.

We are sharing a time here waiting,
husband by her side ticket in her hand.
This is the law.
Her name, Margaret, is called forward.

Does she forget for a moment those
horrible tubes laid over her ears?
Does she for a moment not recall hearing
the slow release of life support?
hoping that last breath was drawn on her own.

She turns her smiling face
wrinkled with age and experience
hair nearing platinum and the hoses,
She turns but does she forget?

This was such a good evening. Its strange and perfect, the circumstances under which we as humans meet each other. Even more fantastic is what we can learn about others and ourselves if only we are receptive. We, through our lives, believe we are so unique and special, and when spontaneous hurt or joy isn't there to bring us together structure is. We tend to use creative categories to separate and distinguish ourselves. I have learned to find joy at being "on the same level" with those around me, I love to see us all as equals. Like magnetism, the extremes of life can push us back to our centers, back to reality and hopefully to compassion and understanding.

I was literally there to respond to a ticket but I was figuratively there to see and connect with people and somehow myself. Margaret through her various life supports had not lost her humanity and that gave me faith in mine. We can still smile and promote positivity in the apparent face of trauma and discomfort. In painful situations more discomfort is the last thing needed or wanted. We should be positive for ourselves and for others. Would I be smiling at my feebleness? Would a broken body bother me if I viewed my life a success? The risk and consequence may have been worth the reward. This is how we might smile though the difficulties of life, by living in a way we consider "worth it".

Document 7 4/16/2009

A feather falling, dusting
down into my perception

asked softly for my attention
and in breaths it was gone.

Gone to capture another imagination
just to be passed and passed.

To catch more weary eyes
to birth more distractions

leading open minds one by one
on little impromptu vacations.

Returning moments after it departs
and youth marches on.

I was in class at college, and the distance between the lecture and myself had been growing. When I noticed a feather drifting into the window that my mind was trying to escape though. My mind raced between "American Beauty" and "Horton Hears a Who". I watched the plumage dance and imagined the message it was sending. It was the titanic going down, cut off from its avian world and being broken down, sinking to the bottom of the atmosphere. My happy distraction left as it came, unexpectedly, and my attention continued to wax and wane. I love a distraction like that. Its like watching a cat play with a toy or a fire burning expressively. We love innocent and curious expression and I think in some way its how we strive to be.

Monday 1/11/2009

Bring on the arrival of doubts
flooding in these early hours.
Each one a small pain,
an attack on your sense of
self-worth.
With beats of your heart
they take hold.
While you are alive they ache,
ache for some justification
some reassurance that all
of this trying or milling about
our existence will deliver you
to some safer place,
warm and in the embrace of eyes
as kind as arms.
Early morning hours are honesty.
These wants and longings are true
in ways you wish you could be honest with
yourself.
Bring them on and see if a collapse can hold me.
Bring them on like floods and thunder,
each is pain and while you are alive it aches.
Bring on this early morning.

This was basically me having a little self pity thinking about all the effort I was putting into life in the name of getting ahead. Was it worth it? What does that even mean? What would it be worth, if it were worth anything? This line of questioning brought me to wonder what outcome was worth something and, what was that something. Effort is an umbrella term for my actions, so what actions of mine does my desired outcome require?

I didn't know what I wanted then and I'm still working it out but I think differently now. I stopped pretending I know and started feeling it more and using my likes and dislikes to guide me, always keeping an open mind. I realized challenges are to be met head on. That doesn't mean there is a collision but it does mean you have to turn and face them. You meet them with faith that if you put in the effort, if you act, the situation will change. Cause and effect. What cause will you effect? How can that cause be effected? What effect do you wish to have on the cause? What effect do you wish it to have on you? Different questions give you different perspectives and that helps dial you in but you must be open and diverse with them.

Class #26 April 19th

White shoes on black pants and jacket,
tape recorders scattered
all ready to repeat verbatim belched
by PHDs and heads of class.
A slew of mispronunciation of person,
labels handed down and given.
He fumbles again.
Roll call complete the aged and learned hand
grips the cream colored chalk.
The high-pitched squeak resumes.
Quick clicking reveals the formation of words
dictated as we turn from students to scribes.
"Knowledge" in black and blue, ink and graphite,
anything to keep the thought preserved,
although abbreviated.
And we nod off in the routine of it all.

I think this pretty well sums up why school was not my favorite place. I assume I am intelligent and believe that I am hardworking and sociable but that method of transferring information was so frustrating to me. I did not like taking on the backwards way being an indentured dept servant and somewhere along the way we became cash cows. Working to pay bills and saving all our time and money for "vacation" to forget about how pointless it all seems and how bored we are. This is our hazing process, another rite of passage on Jacob's ladder climbing towards an imaginary American dream.

Daylight Savings

You would start on the steps and
tread awkwardly to the left
at the nagging wind's request.
Then slip at the first step,
deep and unexpected
stumble after stumble,
each wrench of the body
hoping to regain balance.
But you are at the mercy of your clumsy self.
Still tired those eyes half closed,
the beat of your heart accelerating.

You hit the last step
in a small sigh of relief
yet your startled fingers
cling securely to the railing.
Breathing quick nervous breaths
when on this particular event
a curious sort of smile creeps
just half way across your face.
Awake now you are off,
to clumsily face the day.

Fall back, Spring ahead! I've always thought changing our clocks was such a weird thing. I know the time appears to change with the seasons, the days get longer and shorter and so we must adjust. Its just strange to me that our fix was to slap an hour increment on life and reinforce strict schedules and rigid structure. Like all things Time is relative. Its relative to our enjoyment or despair, to temperature, to daylight, and also relative to the difficulty of the task. Our perception of our time in both length and quality seems to come from expectations we have and reflections we make. All that aside time is change, and change is adjustment and transition and we rarely are open to, or ready for it! Life is the ultimate practice of balance so that we don't irreparably fall apart when our perception of our time catches us off guard or gets us down.

April Afternoon 4/7/2006

Brittle sticks in the daylight
laden now with dew drops,
to the point of strong bows breaking
a breeze pulling gently on your eyes.

Dropped into the lul of an April afternoon.
A perceptive ear could hear the rain drops
scatter as they hit the ground,
one violent explosion after another.
Beautiful acts of demolition.

Yet to touch them to your skin
what bliss when the sun is not piercing.
If only there wasn't this whisper,
some secret on the lips of the air
ringing in a change of heart.

Left to awe at some infatuation
obsessing with each new drop
falling in love with their innocence,
falling apart at their end.

Brittle hearted in some afternoon hour
laden with lovers all since long gone.
this breeze pulling gently on your eyes
dropped into the lul of an April afternoon.

I don't specifically recall the day that inspired this but I do remember the feeling. It was an afternoon caught between seasons, somehow snowing and raining and evaporating at the same time. I was sitting on the porch looking out across the field just experiencing the world happening around me. It was almost sad to see winter leaving, but I felt like the trees – bent and pushed to my limit. Winter is our great metaphor for hardship. Even though spring may be on it's way, transition is hard but necessary. I have felt the same season on my heart through love. The newness and excitement, the romance and affection, the weakening, and the falling out.

What I have learned since is that the seasons do not stop but their focus and intensity fluctuates and, like nature, if you understand them and become familiar with them they aren't so bad. We can be very hard on ourselves and this can make us unforgiving. If you cannot forgive yourself and be kind to yourself then you cannot do that for others. This is where we get stuck in a closed loop system. Our inability to be grateful for and forgive ourselves prevents us from being grateful for and forgiving to others which is desperately needed. Gratitude and Love are the Yin and Yang of life. Looking back and reading this I recognize the path I have been on and why I choose to walk it.

A Syllable Cycle of Life 12/15/2019

I.

I am-
The one who IS-
The one who will be for all time.
To what life my mind has birthed
my body gives form.

I will die.
I struggle with my fate.
I try not to lose faith in myself.

Body gives its life
for mind to become alive.
The mind that will be for all time.
The thing that IS-
unbound-
Free.

An absolute possibility
so try and try again
for all time.

This is the most recently written piece included is this book. It was structurally inspired by numerology. The syllables go 1,2,4,8,7,5 – 3,6,9 – 5,7,8,4,2,1 – 9,6,3 and bounce from spirituality to actuality, from the mortal dilemma of death to the spiritual question - if the spark doesn't just vanish, where does mine go when my body can no longer contain it? Through some reading into the idea that numbers can represent more than just quantities I wondered what all the numbers ancestrally meant.

Of all the numbers 3,6, and 9 sparked this, they are to be considered metaphysical numbers. The idea is 3 represents pure matter, thoughtless potential. 9 represents pure thought, the inspiration for all life. The number 6 is life, it is where thought meets form. Look at a Yin Yang and 9 as the light part, 3 as the dark, 6 would be the line between the two. It is the path of life with a foot on either side represented by the eyes in the design. I thought I'd toss in some doodles of mine making associations with numbers and colors, elements, day and night, male and female. Then turn those numbers into shapes or patterns which can be pretty cool.

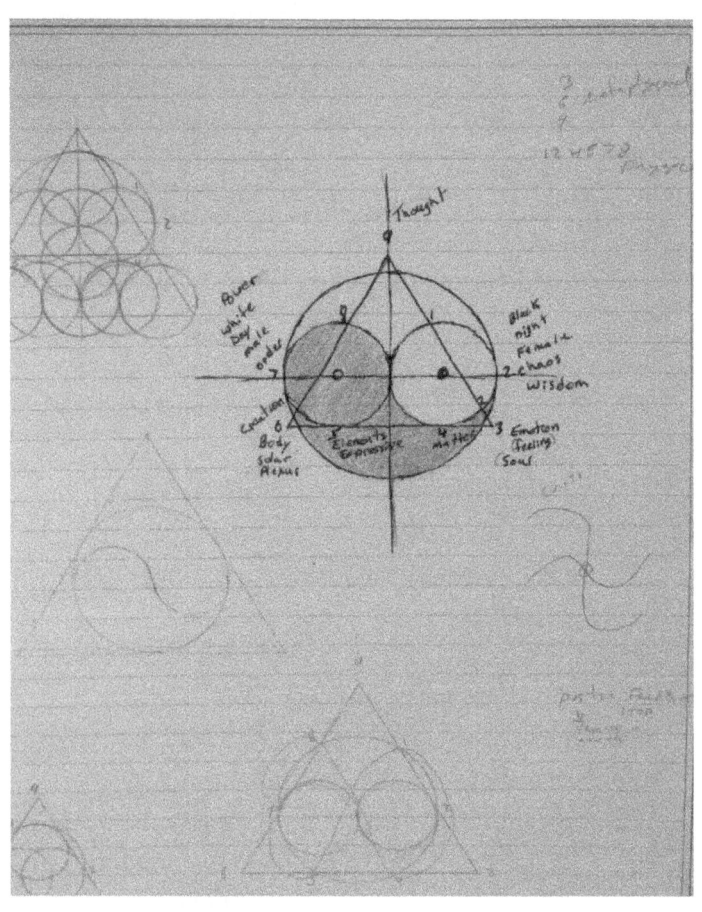

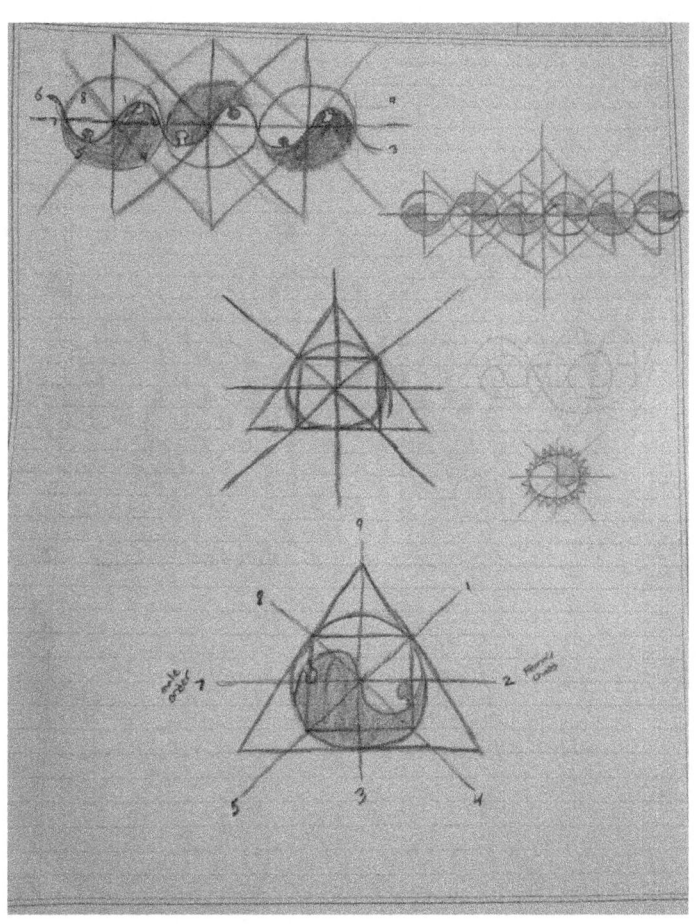

Thoughts

Introspection 5/29/2017

Strange is my time
when I am trading
memories for wisdom
my experiences for all knowing
I trade my specific recollection
for compassionate recognition
growing fuller for all time.

It can be confusing when our values or our tastes change and in transition we cling to old habits. We are constantly changing and reconciling that change, trying to understand what it means three- fold; what it means about us in the past, what what it means for us now, and what it will mean for our future-self. Change is a broad term and often threatening, suggesting some discomfort. I see change as what we anticipate it to be and what we make of it. Change is raw neutral and absolute. We give it definition and translation. We should not be blind to it and collide with it increasing the severity of its impact. Birth is life, life is change, change is opportunity, opportunity is birth.

The Truth... as I recall it

I have, in my years thus far
come to realize
that I am a King,
a God,
among Gods on this earth
who consistently fail
to realize themselves.

The truth... as I recall it
is that I am a force.
I am absolute
and though my stories
may embellish
my truths can create
universes.

The truth ... as I recall it
is I was thrown
both into life
and across a
strangers kitchen table
by my cousin,
igniting a whole house brawl
that ended with
an oven ding
followed by corn beef hash.

The truth... as I recall it
is that I drove myself, my father
and three others who

will not be named
down a washed out ravine
in a golf cart
on an intoxicated full moon night.

The truth... as I recall it
is that I
in the youth of my human life
have loved so completely
I could go the rest
without.

The truth is
I am God
I am all powerful
and that is not perfection.
I am not perfect.
But what Gods are
may cast the first stone.

"But just because its honest, well that doesn't make it true" Lyrics from the song Wilderness by Middle Brother. My hope and thought for my life is that I can be both honest and true.

Attentive not obsessive

Mail goes on the counter
by the phone.
Salt and pepper shakers
belong next to the napkins
and my acorn
always goes in my right
front pocket.

I like to put misplaced things
back in the same place
each time so that at least
I know where it was last
and in hopes it gets a home
and that others will
catch on.

I put the toe nail clippers
back into the medicine cabinet
every time I find them
on the arm of the couch,
or by the sink in the kitchen,
or even when they have made it
as close as the counter
underneath of the cabinet,
two feet from their
half-way house.

Sometimes I slack
and it takes a longer time
away from home.

I tend to be that way
with myself too.

I try to always remember
to put myself back home,
back into my medicine cabinet
ready to let proximity
heal and smooth over
the rough parts in my spirit
feeling worn from
a hard walk about.
Eternally worn
but eternally headed toward
home.
I expend I accumulate
all is new all is the same.

Just a day

Today may be counted as all the days before it,
just a day.
One filled with attempts and dreams
swelled to burst with so many thoughts,
secrets, so many whispers and longings,
so much time.
So much air to be breathed and
breathed slowly taking the time to savor
life as it happens,
history in the making, our own history.
We make plans and dates and deadlines so
quickly,
and why not impressions?
Why not moments that leave us laughing,
leave us enamored by the fact that
we can make differences?
These moments when we are not
talking or living for paychecks.
When we are not taking steps towards
ends or destinations,
but people.
Taking chances at something better
not playing it safe or holding to
closely to these tall tall buildings,
holding to fears that in the end
this truly makes no difference.
Today is just a day.

I do not want to see us, as humans, lose our empathetic knowledge though vain individuality. We want to look different, act different, sound different, feel different and this unjustifiable want can convince us that we are different. Did we forget about relativity? I understand our need for individuality. We need to be valued as individuals. Love for our fellow people was dying, and when no one is valuing you it is hard to value yourself. Enter individualism a small band aid for a large problem birthed from high demands of production and population explosion.

My family taught me the true value of self, which is not the ego. True value of self is not my idea of me, it is my skills and knowledge as I apply them to that around me. We as people are reference points for each other and you lose your mind as well as place in society trying to scream your individuality. We are so busy saying look at how different I am and being self absorbed we fail to see the value in others. We even resort to comparing whose pain is worse. It is difficult to see past our own opinions, either we can all be right to some degree or we can all be 100% wrong. How do you fit someone who views things differently than you into your world, not with pity or contempt but with love?

Priorities 6/3/14

My run in with addiction
left me with constant reminders
of what my life used to be.
I've been coke heads
with bad teeth.
I've been heroine addicts
walking through trips
like zombies.
I've been a baby like Eli
meeting this world so innocent.
Through love and a little fear
for my life
I broke though my addictions.
Traded my material pride
for my spiritual worth
and it has left me with constant
reminders of what my life
used to be.

The more people I meet the more problems I see swept under the rug, creating many un-dealt with trip hazards in the fabric of our time in space. I see unaddressed issues everywhere and we are all paying the price. We suffer from fear of facing our reality, our weakness overall is our aversion to discomfort. We are constantly looking for ways to escape it. Aren't we? Through drugs, alcohol, solitude, judgement, possession, even death.

The world is a beautiful, wonderful place if you look around were people don't get involved much. The world of nature is a neutral place and in it we humans have developed the ability to be consciously negligent. We can know what we should do - without knowing the compulsion to do it. That is, knowing which action is right and not doing it.

Racket Inside-Out

Do you ever get tired
of being so loud?
All the sounds we make
all the noise, noise
women in their heels
click click clicking,
people on their phones
shouting always shouting.
It seems these days
we do not even
breathe quietly.
We gasp through mouths
full of food
we interrupt gossip
with more of the pointless same,
obsessed with all of the
noise we can make.
Do you ever get tired
of being so loud?
The music in the car,
your t-shirts and designer jeans,
your life bangs on
like some awkward gong
Slam Slam Slam Slam.
Volume up, Humanity down.

I remember being in high school and being very aware of how concerned people were with brands and labels. You get graded on everything, overtly and covertly. I was of the mind to try and fly under all radars if possible. I didn't insist on trendy clothes. I didn't shoot for the highest grades. As long as I felt I understood, to the best of my abilities, the mark I received was irrelevant. When it comes to clothes I wouldn't wear anything with a logo. I withdrew myself from that quiet competition not wanting that to be anyone's first judgement of me.

Either my clothes would be clean or dirty but keeping brand-less was key. It is hard to achieve balance and live on, what I realized was very unstable and biased ground. Our want to be accepted means that we are giving others power over us in terms of having to accept us. Which opens the door to all sorts of scrutiny and so many strings attached to compliments and favours we become puppets. When I was young it was just clothes, now its everything you own or do that seems to come with extra outside input.

I try to be completely myself now and to not need or want to make someone think something about me before they have met the actual me. I try not to be loud. I try to be quiet, perceptive,and receptive. I try to be my own filter for all life's man-made garbage.

<u>I think, I try, I create</u> 5/12/15

I am an experimental being.
I have projects to this day
in all forms of their production,
a range from rough drafts
on rest-stop diner napkins
to perfect completion in the
form of duct work hanging
elegantly in the under
appreciated basement of a
house that you will never see.
I am thinking, trying, creating.
Always.
On the way to creating
often things go unfinished
given up in search for
perfection.
I want perfection in all things
so I think, I try, I create.

On the path to self-improvement and discovery I realized the answer to health was youth and newness. Information to support this is all over now, we need to do new things and explore and learn. New thoughts and experiences are what will keep us youthful. I may not look like my 15 year old self but I feel like him, only now I have more insight. I have age and, hopefully, wisdom. The former I acquired naturally the later, gradually, with open mind and thought.

Creativity is like working out, in the beginning all your motions are stiff and unfamiliar. Then gradually you get more and more able and your ability will birth curiosity. If what was difficult isn't now, what is the new level of difficulty? What is the new challenge presented by progress? Most of what I do ends up scrapped, and I think that's how creation is. Ninety-nine ideas discarded for one fantastic success which is relative, subjective, and individual – internal. My points are - keep trying, quality over quantity, and go easy on yourself.

Grandma B. 11/23/2009

We take our memories for granted
faces and names are easily recalled
summoned up ready to let us relive
moments or days in our past.

We take for granted remembering dates,
falls springs and mornings.
Remembering the touches of people
who spent moments in our lives
then pass either on or by
to exist only in our thoughts and dreams.

Watching this thing fade in her
tears at me and would pull up
all of my most cherished memories.
What would I do if they began to fade
slipping away small details at a time?

She now needs dates
on the backs of photographs
names by row in family albums
it aches in my chest
to see the struggle in her eyes
trying desperately not to be empty.

The people she loved and still loves
step slowly from her mind and blur.
Phantom aches from time forgotten
how hard it must be this forgetting.

Getting old doesn't bother me really and neither does the thought of death or conclusion of this life. What does make me sad is acknowledging that I won't get to keep all my memories or my able body for my whole life. Natural death is a result of weakness and it is scary to be weak, scary to depend on others. My great grandma died feeble and yet graceful. Her weakness became our strength as we all became part of the process of her passing on. It is unavoidably sad to consciously acknowledge forthcoming fate, but it is necessary and liberating. The sadness may not retreat but the weight of it goes away and allows you to move past being selfishly sad towards being grateful.

Something Better

In all these tests and rules,
in these trials, these lives
we need to find our space
to breathe and be, to blossom
disregarding these prefabricates.
We are not parts.
We are wholes.
We are something larger,
something waiting to be.
Waiting to bloom
to come into acceptance,
to revel and laugh
so deep chested that
we breathe in the winds of change
and we beam, oh we beam
the most true and brilliant colors.
We need to find ourselves,
and in life where is the time?
Where is the time to stop and breathe?
Where is the time to prove we are
something different, something better?
Where is our time to be?

It seems the search for piece of mind and contentedness has driven many movements and sparked routines, rituals, and religions. The only thing that stands out and seems to be important across the spectrum is us spending "quality" time with each other. Quality here to be understood as meaningful time, time spent with focus on a common task or in a common direction, allowing and expecting all participators to wantingly contribute. Then personal opinion and industry stepped in and made our little world rock. It wobbles from individualism, to culturalism, then spiritualism.

Each one as an extreme is out of balance and it could be our task to calm the waters and re-balance these pillars of what I believe to be US. Right now our culture is struggling with individuality and spirituality because we as people are running and judging everywhere. We long for the comfort of a group where we can be free natured and have faith without stones being cast from within our own supposed tribe.

Taking responsibility

Our bodies have been longing for peace
in this Evolving and Cycling world.
Our minds have lost their social skills
in the midst of so much
Distraction and Discrimination.
Our monuments are testaments
not to our accepting nature,
but to our conquesting abilities.
We are not to judge,
now or ever.
There has been and
will continue to be,
as far as trends will tell us,
our inability to live with
and tolerate ourselves.
So, who is to blame?

Aside

We grow up so much faster than we plan to. We get rushed by people to make decisions that we're not sure we are ready for, just because *they* were rushed to do the same. We pass on stress and somewhere along the way we got the idea that we had to do so much. We have to go to school and work and shake hands and smile and somehow keep it all in check. We have to keep it all in some sort of rhythm, this impossible measure that rarely syncs up with our wild emotions.

The steps we take are awkward and unsure; one forward, two back, and three to the side. Our stopping point is never where we thought it would be and people tell you all of the things that you need to be happy. Have they really got it that figured out? I am not convinced. We make life so complicated, and for no reason at all. Get better grades, get a better job, get a better house, get a better car. But is that what life is, just - get a better something?

Acquire all those things, those expensive material things, waste your life for dollar signs and just before you go to sleep I bet you miss life's simplicity. Like sitting on broken couches watching small off color television sets and drinking cheap beer with your friends. These are the things you find yourself missing when you are tied to work or waiting in traffic always running late.

You miss the road trips and not having any money... or cares, and you miss the closeness that you came to fall in love with.

You will find that suits and fancy cars and offices are stale, boasting an air of predictability. Do all the checks you want for what's missing, search and search and search and I guarantee you one thing, your heart is nowhere to be found. Life is about where your heart is and it can change as people change and last and be pressured but it can also be lost. So take your tests and take your chances, but don't forget to take your time. And home will be there just the way that you left it.

Homesick

We Wrattens claim the swamp-lands
our territory sectioned off by black rivers
whose swift current has washed me down stream
away from my willow trees and cider press
away from my loves and the smell
of my fathers room.

I have been carried off to Georgia
and seen the clay and stones near Gainesville.
I have drifted through Auburn, Alabama
stealing memories on film as I went.

These tributaries meet estuaries
and at once I am engulfed
in awkward yellow lights and sounds
of terrible beasts that lurk near.

Sirens in the distance as a wake-up call
I wish to be off this asphalt torrent,
car docked near the lilac tree
tethered to the tigerlilys
my side of 20 enjoying the afternoon
buried beneath the clover

>>>

> Hiding deep in Wratten country
> away from the math and ignorance.
> I am honest to the air I breathe
> and to the dirt beneath my feet.
> They have given me life and I
> have allowed them to see the world.

> But I will be home soon and this body
> will return itself and surrender,
> giving back to Wratten Land.

    I worked once as a traveling photographer for a company that provided its services to colleges and organizations across the country. While I was with them I would travel for three months at a time, living out of a combination of hotels, my car, thrift stores and gyms. In six months I worked in nineteen states and got a change to see a sizeable chunk of our country and our people. Three pieces from my time traveling ended up in this book - *Homesick*, *Nature vs. Nurture*, and *Perspective*. They were written in that order and made it here in that order.

    I loved getting to travel a bit, seeing and experiencing, developing appreciation for what I had. But I love home too and I had a great one growing up, not just the house but the place. I consider four or five whole towns here as home and the people who fill them as some of the best you will meet.

Earth to Jacob

Angry rebelliousness stirs again
This gut of mine stands up
apart from myself and leaves.
Let the school burn.
Let the teachers lose their Tenure.

Let's go back to sticks and stones,
to barter-trade,
to lighting fires for heat.
Before vegetarians and humanitarians,
state of nature.
Before protesters and lobbyists and whores.

Let these hands of mine be free
to build when inspired
to slam when in anger
never at the mercy of command.
Paying someone else to tell me that
I am smart.

Bring life expectancy back down to 50... Tops!
Keep me the hell off life support.

What we choose to fight,cry, and die for
lacks importance.
Lets give up the red carpet
and labels to our faith.

>>>

When your heart stops and
the afterlife finds you
it won't matter what they believed in.

Stop passing your damn judgement and
bite those hypocritical tongues
until they bleed, now swallow.
Drink that life,
drink blood and hate it
but remember it is keeping you alive.

Oh and think of this!
Something so discouraging
disheartening,
when outside its proper place.
Blood keeps you alive from the inside.
Hate the sight, smell, and taste
but die without it.
Just like our other undesirables,
cleaning vomit and pumping toilets.
They are the blood.
Now swallow.

Whine and cry and bitch and beg
about so much life you will never see
a million abortions you'll never control,
babies that you will never hold.

A billion beaten bodies
with scars your fingers will never touch
mutated children born from dirty war
smoke filled lungs from bombs

but you are helping,
you eat organic.

Now carry on concerned with magazine ads
and the lies that other people live
that will never affect you.
Raising those arms up in outrage,

most always too late.

A Good Person Trying to Be Better

I am a good person trying to be better. It's just that every time I am doing something that I shouldn't be, that is when everyone is watching. They happened to tune into my boring life as I punch a hole in a wall or decide to drive after several drinks. It's like an old guy I used to work with once said: " one aw-man is worth ten at-ta-boys". you can do something right over and over again but the one time you slip is when they're actually paying attention, when it actually matters.

So here I am, stuck trying to find something solid to put my feet on. I just want something constant, something I am sure of, something I can hold. That's what this wanting to be better is all about. I feel like I used to take too much for granted my looks, my way with women. Maybe not keeping in them, but getting them I seem to have no problem with.

I was never good enough to my family especially my dad who would have bent over backward for me and then some. He was lucky if I called once a month to see how he was. The nice I was to people was fake which felt strange because I wanted to be nice deep down but the facade I put on was not genuine.

I simply wanted to much. I wanted to be attractive and desired in any way that I could be. I wanted people to fall for me. I wanted people to love me and potentially be crushed if I stepped out of their lives but still keep on loving me. This is the process of confession after all these years of trying to fool myself. This is repenting, a change in my direction. I wanted to be perfect so badly, perfect for everyone. The trouble is that I lost myself under so many additions and changes of clothes. That's when you find someone who catches you off-guard and shows some real interest and you get scared. You scramble for some new mask to afraid to risk seeing if they like the man behind it.

I need to be better for women, for the women who I care about, for that which is feminine. Masculinity is not the problem but in all its computations it forgets and sets aside emotion for results. I am breaking and merging these two sides of me, and I have stopped trying to be "perfect". There's no such thing as perfect and I am not trying to fool myself any longer. I want to argue and get mad and be corrected when I make mistakes. I want to keep learning and be humble and thankful to the people who enrich my life.

So here I go uprooting the edge of my comfort zone, where parts of me pull in all directions making it difficult to move forward. I want to be done with pretending. I want people to know me and I want to apologize for years of not trying to be myself, for fear of being rejected.

I am a good person but I want to BE a good person too. I want to be human now and not some image crafted from surveys and focus groups to be a more reliable consumer. I want to be my awkward self and let my friendships and relationships speak for me. No more excuses or trying to make up for things that I have imagined I lack. I am a good person trying to be better. This is me.

Self Discovery

All the weight of my actions,
I can feel.
Each one tethered
to some invisible Eternity thread
bound to the fabric of me.
I am all of my choices
all of my rights
all of my wrongs,
and on some nights
all of those strings
pull together,
towing me out
of this earthly harbor
to venture honestly
into open spiritual waters.

It has become apparent to me how important reflecting is. We should look back at our decisions and interactions and speculate on their appropriateness. I no longer think that I am right in any given situation but I look forward to reflecting on it, how I felt during it and whether or not I feel good about the result. I am internally, mentally honest and open with myself and give heartfelt criticism and encouragement. I love being open with myself and challenging myself, playing devils advocate and determining if how I feel holds up to my own scrutiny. I do this also spiritually. What do you think? Why do you think it? Why is it important for you to think that? What does it do for you? What do you for it? Like the *who, what, when, where, how,* and sometimes *why* of journalism, I dig for facts through meditation.

Nature vs. Nurture

I was raised civilized
but I can be primal.
I can smile
and I can be violent
or I can do both,
at the same time.

Sometimes I want to use my hands and my teeth and rip and tear and slaughter. Sometimes I want to be the animal society has tried to teach us to forget, tell us that we are not. Well society, biology tells me something different. It tells me that I share genetics with monkeys and dolphins and rats!

I was raised Primal
but I can be civilized.
I can be violent
and I can smile.
Or I can do both
at the same time.

I was raised wild and I use my meat teeth and my cunning. I use my body in unison with my mind because they are not separate. I use them to track, kill, and trick. I use them to survive, just as we have been since the beginning. Since the first bit of matter tore itself in two.

>>>

> I was raised for hardship
> but I was borne to smile.
> I can laugh
> and I can cry
> or I can do both
> at the same time.

Sometimes I can't eat as much as I should and my frame thins, but this is life. I must fast like the rest of life does, like a bear or snake or a blood-sucking tick. I rest and slow down and let my body do what it does, I let my adaptations work and I do not fret. Because this is life, and it is not always easy.

> I was raised to smile
> but I was borne for hardship.
> I can cry
> and I can laugh
> or I can do both
> at the same time.

I choose to look up in life, to hold my chin high and keep my eyes open. We do have a choice and it is mine to face all of this being alive with a grin on my stupid face. All the while keeping my back and constitution strong. Using these shoulders of mine to carry on and on and on. My heart forever alight.

Document 6

Cracks cracks and always cracking.
My hands bleed around protruding knuckles
the blood pools just inside my palms.
My legs are aching now and will forever.
This crown of tears, sweat, and fortitude begs
asking gently for permission to rest
these many aching inquiries,
that they may have moments to play catch up,
to call out the names of those who
should not have been forgotten.
Only good for dragging out old smiles,
stirring up old conversations
which remind us why they are gone.
You are the only one who understands
how darkness can be friendly,
and you whisper don't be rash boy.

Still Boys 9/10/2009

Still boys after all the growing up we've done,
our youth invested in skills we still use.
15-year-olds built cabins and dams and get-a-ways,
now entering our twenties we build bars and walls.

We build our foundations after years of planning.
And we are still boys, not quite yet independent
trying desperately to take hold of life
busy making impressions, retreating when we need to.

Tired of user friendly applications and
how much more we genuinely seem to care than
so many others of our generation,
one raised to point fingers and place blame and cry.

These "Boys" will stand up and take the accusations
take the responsibility to carry more than our fair load.
Safe to say we are as important as a spine.
We don't take charge but we help a body stand.

Still boys after all the growing that we have done
keeping our youths protected and fiercely guarded,
this thing, this holy thing we have - our memories,
golden afternoons, things we did with our own hands.

We built and laughed and carried and loved
and now we cherish and hold and know consequence.

Intimacy

Document 3

Deep breath now love as this world spins,
we lose our grip and faith at times
but reach for my fingers,
my memory stored somewhere
inside that mind I fell in love with,
know that I am not far.

This body is tired from living
tired from the trying nature
that it seems life can posses,
but it has enough yet to reach you
no matter what this distance is.

That smile is what guides me
your very laugh is my energy.
With it I can stand with more than the weight
of this small world on my shoulders.
Yet give me your dissatisfaction and
my knees would buckle
my hands would no longer hold steady
and I would be washed away
by any distraction that would have me.

So come to me love, call to me.
I am here should you need me
waiting for a whisper or
the touch of your skin,
to live for your smile and laughter.

I dance

I dance when I'm walking,
to life - to this experience
of being alive.
Every step is a note,
every one out of place
was a lesson
as I learn my way
though this improve.

I dance when
I am sweeping the kitchen,
around chairs and backpacks
and sisters.

I dance when
I am helping at work,
around people and pets
and computers.

The tempo changes and builds
like the beat on some great drum
faster and faster and faster
the notes come so quickly
that you miss a few and trip

through the next couple quatrains,
through a job you hate
some late bills and
a little wild hard living.

>>>

Stumble out of
a few bad relationships
and finally, finally
Finally in tune with yourself.
A harmony you have not learned yet,
a music from within,
from around.

I dance when I pass
by you on the street,
when I storm out of a room
and like it or not
you are part of my dance,
and you are perfect.

Love Lasting 2018

We saw ourselves in intervals
Slowly testing the waters
exposing small pieces of our
sensitive souls.
Hoping in such a great and
reserved amounts
that the minds we have progressed to
are ready to fully accept and appreciate,
to love completely as to exist,
each other.
When this time is upon me I will know.
As I knew life was upon me and
as I know death will someday
be upon me.
But you are worth that my lady.
All this patience is yours,
to test as you wish
with your young and beautiful heart
and if you love me
as in my heart I believe you do
then you will play this game with me,
and we will take our time to bloom.

I wrote *Love Lasting* for my wife Jenna, written for her - about Us. Its about Us as I saw Us and how I felt about our relationship and the length of time and distances between us. Making me always wonder when we would see each other again, and if that time would be the one where we finally were together. I felt like the song "Blue Eyes" by Middle Brother:

> "Told myself that you're the one
> And I told myself I could get you back
> When I came back you still weren't mine
> Then I left again and you still weren't mine
> I'm back again so just be mine
> I am so tired of runnin'."

Jenna has brown eyes, so the song title was off but I got the point. It can be scary wanting to be with someone, to love someone. I wanted her to know that I wasn't afraid, not of time, not of distance and not of our differences.

We met in college in 2009 and went back and forth for about ten years. Trying breaking up, being just friends, probably hating each other, and constantly feeling that sometime would be right. We would just have to keep in touch and keep talking and growing as individuals before we were right for a relationship with each other. We are loving opposites finally sensible enough to talk with compassion and understanding.

Only Slowly Goes This 6/28/2009

Only slowly goes this.
Small slips of shoes,
toes bent still in resistance
pulled in inches just imagined miles
counted in heart beats
that echo through your chest.

Only slowly goes this.
How much harder it is
when your heart gets a say
and you keep on with glances,
over one shoulder, then the other
waiting to feel a push.

Only slowly goes this,
as kisses become common place
and the touch of their hand becomes familiar.
Your shyness starts to break and fade
and those slips of your clumsy feet
slow and cease to exist.

Only slowly goes this
resting on exhales,
resting in between your fingers and thoughts
while your arms hold and your words calm,
and you exist
like you never before dreamed you could.

The Good Love 10/15/2009

You fall in love with their flaws,
their imperfections.

One trip at a time
awkward step after awkward step.
Fall in love with all the stubbed toes,
the jammed fingers and colds and
morning voices.

Days welcomed in by burned breakfast,
cold showers because they take too long,
and their knack for making you late.

This is the love that lasts.
This love is true and breeds smiles,
brings nights spent laughing when sleep
is just deemed unimportant when compared.
This love will hold out against hard times,
against bad moods and arguments.

When all the time is quality time
and anger is just pretend.
You fall in love with spilled milk
and forgetfulness and you adore
their crooked teeth and uneven ears.
You fall in love under blankets
fighting about who has more,
pushing buttons just because you can.

This is love when you fall
for every ounce of who they are.
You love all the missed kisses
that only catch half of your lips,
and putting them to bed.
You love falling asleep,
knowing they will be there in the morning.

Love Eternal

I will not keep
my love for you
in this body
in this heart.

They are but flesh,
with time they will fail.
They will pass and decay
and one day cease to be.

But my love will last.
My love is infinite
it will last forever
beyond reason.

My love will last
beyond time I can fathom
and will be kept for you,
safe in eternity.

There to last not as
an emotion or a feeling
but as a thing,
a tangible hold-able thing.

So that when life
bursts and starts anew
its essence will be there
always to be searched for,

for us to find
and know again
on in that way
forever.

The love I have for you
will not live in my heart
a heart of muscles
fibers and cells.

It is not the heart
that is special dear
it is you and
all the parts of me knows it

each of my cells know
your name and your soul
and in all forms I take
I will remember.

Lessons

Story of my life

In the story of my life
I am Jacob,
or I am Jake
when I am not being intimate.
In this story of my life
my car keys are iconic,
a mess of bent lock picks and rings.
Their nature brought about
by my impatience.
In the story of my life
I am both the cause
and the effect.
I make my own waves
just to ride out the storm.
I am my life's creative source
and I am giving it my all,
moving and creating ,
learning and understanding.
Letting my imprint on time be lasting

This is Growing up

This is growing up.
I am growing up and it's hard,
watching aunts and uncles, father, mother
all growing older, my family and
I'm supposed to carry on.
We, we are the next generation.
We are receiving all these responsibilities
little things,
make the bed, cook dinner, clean the house
and BIG things,
the bills are due, 40-plus hour work weeks
kids... kids.
teaching them, feeding them, loving them
even when they knock your mother's lamp
off of the table and send it into
ten thousand tiny pieces
all across the floor
of the house you'll be paying for
well into your middle ages.
This is growing up.
I am growing up and it's frustrating.
Find love, find someone who
you can be with and hold
when this life has all but consumed you,
to hold when it's good and to let them know
that they have made this complete.

Find someone to kiss,
kiss them even when they are mad;
when their boss flies off the handle
or right in the middle of a mid-life crisis.
Find someone you can wake up next to
everyday and know why you work so hard
and why you come home after long days
just looking forward to seeing their face.
and when you do find that don't give up.
Don't regret, do not regret anything,
take chances and prove to them
you are worth something.

Do it for everyone who has given up
or merely settled.
Do it for all those movies you watch
and cry every time they run
into each others arms.
Do it for love itself.
And you can grow up together and pay bills
and argue over chores and
changing diapers and laugh.
Laugh as much as you can because
this *is* growing up.

I can cause seizures.

I am a drawing waiting patiently,
this is unreflecting and I am sorry.

I am not curious anymore – non inquisitive,
I just keep getting handed pages and pages.

In college its not advanced just annoying.
<u>It</u> doesn't feel and why should <u>It</u>?

These words are just graffiti on clean paper
I am defacing private property for no reaction,
only to aid in my recollection methods.

This is society and I am surviving
overtly expressing my own regrets on caffeine.

I am discussing, digesting, I am taking in.
we are absorbent by nature and dying.

Do not distress, I have learned that
the characteristics of life are not living
and that I am not chained to margins.

You survive on reflex alone
excreting all of your nervousness,
dripping caution until you sleep.

I Can Cause Seizures is continually one of my favorite things to read over again. It sounds obscure but it brings back very specific emotions for me. The first line describes the blank slate that I saw myself as, its almost asks the question "what will this drawing be?". It was me asking "Okay what is coming out? What am I going to write down?". This was an experimental piece. In the first line I was looking for something that the second line told be could not be seen. Then I gave up in the third line, was distracted in the fourth and so on. It bounced from introspection, to college, my writing, my mortality and my freedom.

This piece probably took a few hours or more and a daydream or two to complete. It is made up of little snips about what I was feeling and thinking about, the reactions to my thoughts. When I am writing sometimes the thought comes complete and it flows right out, and sometimes it trickles in slowly, even stopping for a while. The latter of the two is nerve racking. Patience is a strength I am working on, and at this time it was difficult to stay open and calm. I would try not to cling so tightly to an idea that it would wither and disappear.

Perspective 4/24/14

I started in North Brookfield,
on Swamp Road at the last
bend before it's expiration,
Madison County, New York
in late January.
Since then I have crossed
town lines, county lines,
state lines and time zones,
but all that changed was the view.

People walk the same and
people drive the same and
people speak the same.
They speak English, Hindi, Spanish,
they all speak gibberish
when they are drunk.
Their words fall to me
about my feet and around my path,
like leaves or needles from trees,
where only
the exceptional of either
win at gaining my attention.

I have seen this country
from behind glass on it's highways,
and from a hammock
in it's back country.
The locals, the tourists,
the ones who have not yet
made up their minds,

even a branch of Georgia's Frontiersmen
and all that changed was the view.

I have seen this country's mothers
its fathers, its children.
None regular all different.
I have seen its soldiers
grow up and become old.
I have looked them in the eyes.

I have walked next to its youth
with ice cream in Radford, Virginia
and danced with Bloody Mary's
along side its dead,
down the happy sin filled streets
of New Orleans, Louisiana.
And all that changed
was my view.

The best discovery I made working all over is how similar people are, the main divider being how fancy and proper we are, or are not, trying to be. Another downfall, I guess, is our hesitance to open up. Its easier in the short run to judge and separate, but improvement and advancement of society comes from time and working with and trying to understand and tolerate each other.

My Meditation 2/27/2009

I caught the wind today,
the smell of spring and dust
the remnants of expired seasons
still hiding under leaves and foot.

In songs of spirit and life
this spirals up again and
blossoms new love and heart
new appetites and hope.

While these small memories fade
we pace about with our tension
as it loosens up it's hold,
remembering,

we need our time for nothing.

Meditating

My eyes are open now,
my metaphorical eyes.
I can see new colors
shades of moods and dispositions.
My DNA is alive and when I
listen close enough It speaks to me,
vibrating like all of these new colors.
I hear red and I can
feel and touch blue.
I am alive in new ways each moment
with the right combinations
of air and water I am alive.
I am alive in the sense that I am aware.
I know myself now.
I am a frequency, a vibration that
was not lost but is just coming
into my own,
my own, my own.
each movement, each acceptance
each change is my own.

Condensation 1/21/2019

The thought train rarely ceases
it shifts covertly from this to that
from primitive need to future desire
the Mind controls all and is thus,
uncontrollable.
With some dedication and some
simple patience
you may give the mind some true,
rest.
A moment or two spared
just to enjoy the consciousness of
breath that is not somehow threatened.
One peaceful inhale and exhale,
those practiced in these arts learn
savored and balanced is
the most difficult and yet rewarding.
Think but do not worry
you have the power to go with nature,
not against her.
Do not ignore what is noticed.
Always be grateful
understanding you are encouraged
to attempt to better the situation,
the future for yourself, if you wish.
Breathe and be thankful be calm and think.
In this mad world find the routine
add some structure take some chances and
aim true.

I feel like *My Meditation*, *Meditation*, and *Condensation* are my progression of awareness lumped into three parts. When I look back it feels like just few big steps, though I know those are just the crests of waves. Progress comes slowly, quickly and seemingly, not at all. In The Tibetan Book of Living and Dying by Sogyal Rinpoche, I first read the word *Bardo*. Through the description I took it to mean a sort of universal "space between", the space between life and death, between thoughts in your mind, the space between sleeping and waking. A practice I have taken on is recognizing that space between and trying be in it for as long as I can.

The "space between" for me is life. Life is our Bardo between birth and death. To be aware and in control of myself in this space is my goal. So this became my practice - to pay attention, to notice when the food is good and appreciate the people who make my life enjoyable. Also notice and appreciate when things are bad because this is how you give value too and appreciate the good. This reminds me of the book The Hidden Messages in Water by Masaru Emoto. Emoto describes an experiment with a water mixture and the effects his influence on it had.

Basically he had three jars of a rice water mixture, daily he would compliment and appreciate one jar, degrade and yell at the second, and completely ignore the third. What he observed was that the ignored jar fared the worst. Neglect and indifference are the worst treatments of any. They are worse than being outright mean. Think about it, if someone is just mean at you, you can know that and move around them. But what about when people completely ignore you and shun you. The worst punishment we're shown is to be shunned. Think about solitary confinement, *in prison*!

This also reminds me of a study on particles that was done to see what happened when we basically shot a particle at a target. The finding was that individual particles can act as whole waves and that watching them could change their behavior, like the saying perception is reality. That's what awareness is, it is you taking control of your reality. Awareness is the first step. It may not be the hardest and I hope that does not discourage you.

With your body if you are unhealthy, you have to first accept and realize that you are. That is awareness. Then you have to learn about your situation, what your options are. Then you have to act, to take part, to exercise your awareness. And Finally you have to accept the force that matches all the control that you do have, is all the control that you do not have. Choice and chance, nature and nurture, you're perception defining your reality and vice versa.

Office Life

Days in and out spent living.
Laughing when we can,
looking for small recesses
and holding air when it's fresh
with our fingers and our noses.

Tuning out voice after voice
and words twist with our lips
as we smile at our ability
to ignore the noses of life.

Sink back into chairs for days
loosen those noose like collars
and say to hell with all those names.
Names on your paychecks
and sneakers and companies
that you didn't know existed.

Let air fall and wash over you
when rain is not an option,
stuck in office cubicles,
stuck in chairs with wheels
and quirky day by day calendars.
15 minute vacations
to return unsatisfied to the real world.
Break free.

I am Sane

Life is strange and complicated,
some twisted impossible puzzle.
We try and we grab for the answers.
We are Quick aren't we?
Stiff arm and straight minded
proud of all the knowledge we have
but never were a part in finding.

We feed on the souls of others
sprouting justly between shaky footprints
carefully following instructions
slowly weeding out uniqueness
through method, by the
application of treatments and pills.
There can be only one type of mind
stagnant, unfortunate, *Relentless*, and unhappy.
In the midst of a maddening normality,

I am sane.

I will be treated for symptoms I do not have.
I will be cured for a sickness I do not possess.
I will be cleansed in all aspects,
from every angle you see fit,
to take me away from myself.
Life is strange and complicated,
some twisted impossible puzzle
we cry and we pry for the answers.

> We're Quick aren't we?
> We all lead our own followers
> from birth to their deaths
> through life that spirals uncontrollably,
> that burns until we are born or accept
> until we bend or we break,
> are we breaking?
> There can be only one type of mind,
> stagnant, unfortunate, *Relentless*, and unhappy.
> Yet in the midst of this maddening life,
> I am sane.

I feel like the world is going crazy around me sometimes and that persuasion has become corrupt. I read <u>Ways of Growth</u> by Herbert A. Otto and John Mann copyright 1968 recently and it made me think of this. I wrote *I am Sane* maybe six or seven years ago. I was thinking about some of the psych. classes that I have taken and arrived at the conclusion that I am one of us sane people on earth. I realized all the salesman peddling their wears and cures were playing on emotion to affect my decision making. Once I took emotion out of advertising and reconnected with my family and friends my anxiety was gone.

The reason the book reminded me of this piece is that Otto and Mann were involved with the Human Potentialities Research Project and The National Center for the Exploration of Human Potential. They describe group awareness and therapy sessions and exercises to explore the mind. We are starting to do this once again, and are just barely beginning to explain and teach emotion to our young again. I feel we started going backwards after "Woodstock". We stiffened up and all got serious and subdued, with the world torn between military, pharmacy, and peace loving - hard working humans.

    I am Sane and you probably are too, but we're slapped with labels and judgement and become a host for fear and insecurity which leads to poor decision making. My advice to you: mentally remove emotion from the advertising you are exposed to. See and hear the images and words but assess who the advertiser is advertising too, and if you want to be that person. Why are ads now shown with seemingly incapable sales people and consumers? Is that supposed to be us? Not me. I am sane. I walk around barefoot, I howl at the moon, and I understand that hard work and responsibility helped earn me the freedom to do so!

I was a deer once 5/31/17

I was on a hike across the world
from the old farm house by the swamp
up to the new cabin on the hill at camp.

I started upright like a man,
by halfway through my trek
I was hunched and I was slowing,
having grown old and tired
reduced to my knees.

So on I crawled into a clearing,
a deer's bed where I sat and transformed.
I left the field and jumped onto
the first trail I saw and kept climbing.

I was clumsy at first with my new gait,
quickly I learned and picked up the pace
looking at every noise the first time
not the fourth or fifth because
by then I could be dead.

I stopped on a small sunny knoll
to rest and take it all in.
I was visited by a chipmunk
making its rounds through
the late may undergrowth,
in the secret hills New York.

>>>

> I ate grass and I lived
> on the earth, of the earth, as the earth,
> harboring my own little ticks
> co-existing as we should
> taking and giving in proportion
> to the point of death,
> where upon you will have taken
> no more than you leave and
> vice versa.
> I was a deer once
> much like I was a child once.
> Experience is necessary and treasured.

The less you allow your imagination to play and flow, the worse it gets at it. If you don't use it you lose it so to speak. I give myself time and space to let creativity and expression flow, and when I feel inspired I follow it's lead. On this day I was actually on a hike up a hill that bordered a hay field and was grumbling to myself about the trek. All of the sudden I walked into a little space where the timothy (a type of grass grown for hay) had been matted down. It was where a deer had made their bed the night before. I lost all preexisting thought and wondered immediately what it would have been like to be that deer. I followed it's path to their main trail and pretended to be a deer, down on all fours tunneling through the undergrowth.

It was amazing, even just in the change in perspective. It was a new trail I'd never taken, possibly no one had, no human at least. But this was a highway for all sorts of things, not just deer. I had hacked the system somehow by being open, receptive, and looking at things in a different way. By changing and expanding my mind the same thing happened to my physical world. It transformed, it expanded and a layer was lifted offering me this unique view of life that we've grown so far away from. Away from our original home, Earth, no modern materials or problems. Just survival.

The Whole *IS* It's Parts

Look at these fleshy appendages
articulate flagella grown not
to move me but that I may move
that which is around me.
See how they hold this pen behold
how easy they make the English language,
look how fast my mind seems to work.

I was taught and that's all nice
but you can teach anything
and teach it to anyone
but I, I have learned!

What a trick that seems to be
and I have, I admit, some skill
passed along through chromosomes
who's small size is hard to comprehend.

Day after day they change, adapt, and
survive long enough to pass on,
pass on what they have learned,
and what they haven't,
create short-cuts, instincts and pass on.

A pause, a head scratch, a smile
an autobiography made possible
by parts whose sum is equally
great as they themselves are individually.

I had read about life cycles of the cells that make up our body and as I understand it, their life cycles are much shorter than that of the human that embodies them. At the gym during a session a conversation might go like this:

Me(to client): can you jump rope?
Client: Yes!
Me: Awesome! When was the last time you jumped rope?
Client: When I was a *kid*(20+ years ago)
Client attempts to jump rope, cannot, frustrated and confused.
Me: Ok, so you remember how to jump rope but *you* have never actually jumped rope before. This body that you have is not the body that jumped rope when you were 9. That body and those cells have been gone for a long time and what you have is a memory. We have to use that memory to teach this new body.

I remind myself of this all the time, it helps to keep me humble knowing that just because I did something yesterday means little. The progress will fade and reverse if I don't stay focused and on path. Yet all that progress I owe to the complex and short lifespan of the microcosm.

I am the Leprechaun

There are bees inside
the mushroom stump,
there is ginseng in my garden.
I keep secrets tucked
inside tree knots.
I am the Leprechaun
I have my treasure,
I have my tricks
and I am not easy
to catch at my craft
of grounds keeping.
I blend and I melt
smokily into the background
with the ferns and cohosh
and your imagination.
To lay with the plants
that will eventually
hopefully get to eat me.
After all it is only fair
for all the years
they have provided me.

I am a leprechaun the way I am most things, just by a feeling or experience I have. Just like in the earlier piece *I Was a Deer Once*. I've never actually been a deer but I moved like one and I feel that I experienced the world like one. Even if it was only for a minute, I related to the idea of them. With this I started thinking of all the qualities that I might share with a leprechaun if there were such a thing. Introduce this practice to the saying I think therefor I am, and I can be anything.

Document 2 10/11/2014

My emotions wax
and my comprehensible
words wane,
to Fleetwood Mac
in my bedroom.
High on a Saturday morning.
I am aware,
aware un-judgingly of
the demands that
lay down all around me
and I will try
my absolute hardest
to meet them all.
All the unspoken responsibilities
to my sisters
and to my friends,
whom I consider eternal
in my version of this world.
My want to be
better for them all
drives me forward
one lesson, one mistake
one step at a time.

I think on some level we have to exist for other people and their well being. The health and wellness of those around us affects our lives more than we give it credit for. It is a common belief in my circle that you are a combination of the people who you hang around the most. I better my life not just for me, but for you and I try to not flame fires of laziness and gluttony. I try to walk my walk and keep my mouth shut, knowing at any moment I could lose my footing, especially in a world where everyone is watching.

I relate this to the gym in that as you improve in your movements, they progress and get harder, and more help is needed through weakness and bad form. The harder of the two for me to demonstrate or get help with was always my weaknesses. That is because its hard to have some one watch you with the purpose of seeing how you are weak. Walking your walk will become difficult, so surround yourself with people who want you to succeed and in some way help you do so. Then, reciprocate that. Your inner circle may change as you take responsibility for yourself but do not compromise your health and happiness, or theirs.

The Universe 1/23/15

A house that was
under construction
taught me a very
important lesson.
That I, as I am
have already come
to beat the odds.
I am a being
that beats all odds.
We life forms are.
Our existence here
is random,
the time and chances
that we take here
are like dust.
Dust from renovations
drifting through this
endless expanse
of space and house.
we define the objects
that we touch,
that we cling to.
While they in turn
define us.
All the while we exist
with some similarities,
until we are wiped out
in the end.

But,
we my dear
have found ourselves
on a piano stool
in a smokers den,
and we are together.
Until we too are
sponged away.
Put back into
our universe,
tossed back into
this cosmic lottery
waiting for
our odds again.

    We unavoidably grow up and grow out of old ways of life and of being. The trouble is growing your mind with your body, and not clinging to tightly to what was. Allowing change to take place and realizing that you cannot stop the change, but you can influence it. Not only you *can*, but you *should*! This is not a practice life and how can you be satisfied with it if you never participate? My thought is that we are here now and so why not make this place be as good as it can be? Why choose misery over happiness, and by choose I mean subject ourselves to. Are we to distracted or busy or indifferent to bother and recognize how special being alive is?

www.ingramcontent.com/pod-product-compliance
Lightning Source LLC
Chambersburg PA
CBHW020945090426
42736CB00010B/1271